MW01181436

53
Things
Ya Gotta Do
An' See In Da

U.P.

(an' they're free or cheap)

Brian Cabell

53 Things
Ya Gotta Do
An' See In Da U.P.

By Brian Cabell

Published by Up North Press, Marquette, Michigan

Print Coordination, Cover Design and Interior Layout by
Globe Printing, Inc., Ishpeming, MI   www.globeprinting.net

ISBN # 978-0-9826043-2-8
Copyright April 2013

No portion of this publication may be reproduced, reprinted,
or otherwise copied for distribution purposes without express
written permission of the author and publisher.

Photography by Brian Cabell unless otherwise noted.

Additional books available at www.briancabell.com

First things first. If you're looking for the Chamber of Commerce's list of must-see, high-dollar, tourist hot spots in the Upper Peninsula, you've picked up the wrong publication. Slam the book shut, set it down and move along. Nothing to see here.

On the other hand, if you're searching for interesting little adventures and experiences that will enrich your stay in the U.P., then this book may provide some help to you.

53 Things Ya Gotta Do An' See In Da U.P. will be your guide to some of the best known venues in the Upper Peninsula, but it'll also lead you to the more obscure, even offbeat places. Some will have universal appeal, others will have intense interest for only a few of you.

By the way, there's no Disneyworld here in the U.P., no Mall of America, no Grand Canyon. Sorry. Head south, east or west for those attractions.

But these fifty-three are cool places, definitely Yooperish, and most will require some expenditure of time from you–anywhere from a half hour to an entire day. Fortunately, however, most won't require you to shell out much, if any, cash.

Plan on something more than a simple "photo op" at these places. You'll be *doing* rather than just *seeing*. Photographs are fine for Facebook and photo albums but seriously, wouldn't you much rather be experiencing something rather than just documenting your visit for your friends and family back home?

Take some time here, breathe in the fresh air, say hello to some smiling faces, and appreciate the fact that life–minus the usual mind-numbing obsession with money and efficiency–is pretty damn good. That's what the U.P. offers you.

Okay, enough of the social commentary. Read the book, pick the spots you want to visit, and enjoy the Upper Peninsula.

Brian Cabell

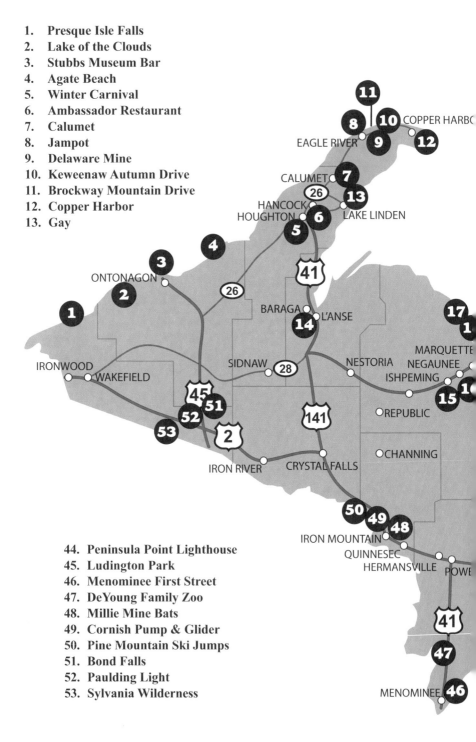

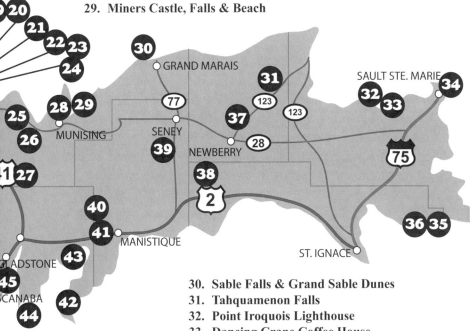

Presque Isle Falls

This isn't as stunning as Pictured Rocks in Alger County, but it's hard to imagine there's any place in the Upper Peninsula more beautiful than Presque Isle Falls on the western end of the Porcupine Mountains Wilderness State Park.

It's got everything a lover of beauty in the outdoors could want.

How about three gorgeous waterfalls plunging onto a shallow, shale riverbed?

How about a swinging footbridge crossing the river?

Or well-maintained trails and boardwalks along the river leading out to Lake Superior?

A beautiful rock and sand beach?

A luxuriant forest featuring maple, birch and hemlock trees, some dating back nearly four centuries?

You can hike here for ten minutes or several hours. The climb will be tough in some places.

A vast sea covered this place a billion years ago. The Ojibwa called it home a couple of centuries ago. Today it's a treasure for regular folks who've escaped the cities and suburbs in search of a gorgeous and accessible outdoor adventure.

You'll need a Recreation Passport to get in. If you've got Rover with you, you'll need to put him on a leash.

Phone: 906-885-5275 (Porcupine Mountains Wilderness State Park)

Directions: Take Highway 519 north until you can't go any farther.

Lake of the Clouds

One of the prettier sights in the U.P.

It's located only a mile or so from Lake Superior on the eastern edge of the Porcupine Mountains Wilderness State Park, about ten miles west of Silver City.

The less ambitious hiker will need to climb only about one hundred yards on a well-maintained path up to a rock cliff that overlooks Lake of the Clouds in the valley below. Take your photographs, peer through the telescope (free!), set yourself down on the smooth rock face and relax. If it's sunny and warm, it's glorious up here.

Hang on to your rambunctious kids. It's a long way down.

You can picnic on the rocks or at picnic tables below, just off the parking lot.

Now, if you're more energetic, try to tackle one of the many trails in the immediate area. They range from three miles to twenty miles or more.

Bring a snack or lunch, water, and good walking shoes.

There's plenty to explore here. This is the largest state park in Michigan.

You'll need a Recreation Passport. Rover will need a leash.

Phone: 906-885-5275 (Porcupine Mountains Wilderness State Park)

Directions: Take Highway 107 west until you can't go any farther.

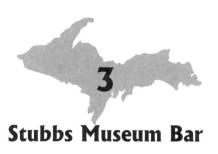

Stubbs Museum Bar

This is a unique combination of bar and museum in Ontonagon, a delightful little town that's been struggling through tough economic times. Companies keep closing down but most of the residents stay on, hoping for a return to prosperity.

Stubbs Bar, in the center of downtown, dates back to the late nineteenth century when the building was a livery stable. It subsequently became an auto repair shop and a grocery store and then finally evolved into the hybrid it is today.

It's a large, darkly lit, friendly bar where, everywhere you look, you'll find souvenirs from the past, including a large, stuffed black bear, along with deer, moose, caribou and buffalo heads, antique rifles and pistols, a leather football helmet, an old slot machine and juke box, countless old beer cans with brand names long-forgotten. And much more.

You could spend an hour here poring over the "museum" pieces while nursing your $2.50 beer.

Stubbs is open every day of the year except for Christmas, 10:30 in the morning until 2:30 in the morning. In other words, it's gonna be open when you stop by.

There are worse ways to wet your whistle.

Phone: 906-884-9972

Address: 500 River Street, Ontonagon

Agate Beach

This is a little off the beaten path (and there's nothing wrong with that) but it's one of the best places in the Upper Peninsula or, for that matter, the United States, to hunt for agates.

You'll be driving on a gravel road the last two miles to the beach–about midway between Houghton and Ontonagon on Lake Superior–and it will leave you at a small, inexpensive campground on a bluff overlooking the beach. Park there.

It's a beautiful tree-lined beach, mostly sandy and littered with driftwood, but at the water's edge, you'll find literally millions of smooth rocks.

Many of them are gorgeous, some are agates. You'll need a discerning eye to identify them, but there's a good chance on warm days you'll find professional rockhounds combing the shore for agates, and they'll be glad to help you determine the difference between a pretty rock and an actual agate.

When winds out of the north whip up the waves, you may have to wade out a bit to find your treasure, but that's part of the fun.

Kids love the challenge. Adult rock-lovers, needless to say, do, too.

Bring a picnic and stay for the day. If you've got fifteen bucks, camp for the night. Rover's welcome.

Directions: Take Misery Bay Road off of M-26, follow sign to Agate Beach.

Winter Carnival

Everybody loves building snowmen, right? But how about snow castles and creatures, when they're maybe twenty feet high with incredible detail and creativity? Well, that's something else.

And that's what you'll find each February at the annual Winter Carnival at Michigan Tech in Houghton. Understand, these aren't a bunch of drunken college yahoos carelessly slapping together some ice and snow. Well, maybe they do drink some beer, but Tech is an engineering school, and the students here take this ice-building thing pretty seriously.

The biggest, most elaborate structures are built over the course of a month; the smaller ones are built in a single night, and of course, prizes are awarded to the best structures. Fraternities, sororities and other campus organizations all take part.

Stroll around the campus during the last days of the competition, or immediately afterward, to get a full appreciation for what these budding engineers can do. Nighttimes are best because lights glisten off the structures. It's a winter wonderland.

Dress warmly, although there have been some winters when the ice-builders have had to struggle with temperatures that climb into the high thirties or even the forties. As they've discovered, you can't build much with forty degree ice.

Web: www.mtu.edu/carnival/

Address: Take US-41 to the campus just east of downtown.

Ambassador Restaurant

The Ambassador Restaurant looks like a classy, atmospheric, turn-of-the-century saloon, the sort of place that Hollywood should have discovered by now.

The wooden bar is l-o-n-n-n-g and polished. Aged wood paneling all around. Stained glass windows. Old-timey light fixtures.

It all takes you back in time. You almost expect to see dirt roads and hitching posts for horses up front.

The big features, though, are huge, whimsical murals of gnomes that cover the walls in much of the bar and restaurant. Strange but enchanting. You're not likely to see anything like this anywhere else in the U.S.

The building is more than a century old and has gradually changed through the years. Now it's a great place in Houghton to stop in for a drink and maybe have a pizza. The food's good and inexpensive. In the back, you've got a commanding view of Portage Lake.

Michigan Tech students love the Ambassador. In fact, some nights, you'll struggle to find anything but students here, and it's a good bet they won't be doing their engineering homework. Or gazing at murals of gnomes.

Phone: 906-482-5054

Website: www.theambassadorhoughton.com

Address: 126 Shelden Avenue, Houghton

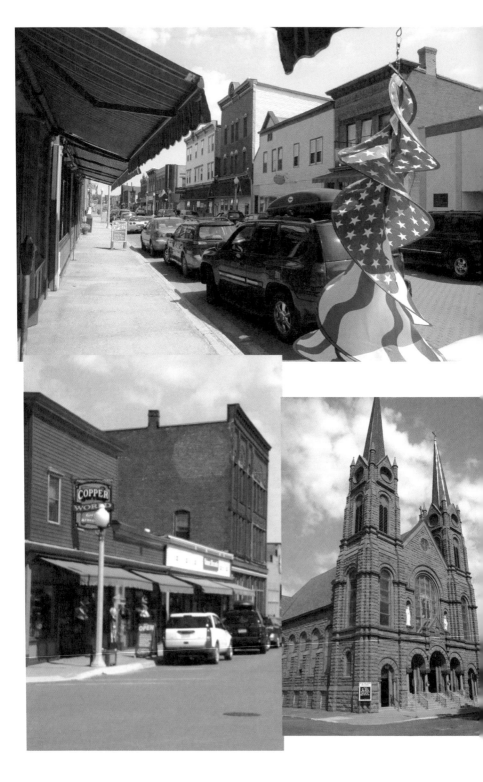

Calumet

This is a town that reeks of history. Take a walk downtown here and you can imagine what it was like to live at the turn-of-the-century in the Upper Peninsula.

This was Copper Town USA, the center of copper mining for all of the country. Almost 5000 people lived here in 1900, more than 25,000 in the surrounding area. Today, Calumet's population barely nudges 800, and there are plenty of empty storefronts.

But there's also the glorious, restored Calumet Theater, the Slovenian sandstone St. Paul the Apostle Church, numerous art galleries, gift shops, coffee shops, restaurants and bars.

Just a leisurely walk through the classy Vertin Gallery makes the trip here worthwhile. It's an unlikely center of major artistic activity.

Many of the shops close up in the winter, but there's life here year-round, and there's a certain Arctic charm to Calumet in the winter.

Be forewarned, though. This ain't Carmel or Santa Fe, all fancy and precious and pricey. This is a town that could have died decades ago after the copper mines closed down, but it's persevered and is slowly showing signs of coming back, thanks to folks who don't mind the cold and absolutely love the arts.

Directions: Take US-41 fifteen minutes north of Hancock, follow the sign to downtown.

Phone: 906-337-6246 (Main Street Calumet)

Jampot

This little store on M-26 east of Eagle River has reached nearly legendary status.

Among its offerings: high brush cranberry jelly, wild rosehip jam, blueberry brandied peach preserves, and wild pincherry jelly. You'll also find cookies, breads, truffles and muffins, one of which could feed a family of four and still provide leftovers for a snack on the road.

The monks of the Society of St. John first came here in 1983 and built their monastery on the other side of the road. It's beautiful, surrounded by a lush garden. The Jampot was opened a few years later, and now six monks are running a thriving operation.

You won't find many businesses in the U.S. where the man behind the cash register is a robed monk. But don't worry, they're just regular folks. They smile and chat about the weather, just like the rest of us.

The Jampot coordinates its opening around the time of Michigan Tech's graduation, usually in late April, and it closes at the end of the color season in the Keweenaw. It's closed on Sundays.

If you're interested in the chapel at the monastery across the street, you're welcome at Vespers on Saturday afternoon, and at services on Sunday morning. The building's not a cathedral, though. You may find yourself having to stand for the entire service.

Website: www.societystjohn.com/store/   (no phone)

Address: 6559 State Highway M-26, three miles east of Eagle River, five miles west of Eagle Harbor.

9
Delaware Mine

You can't talk about the history of the Upper Peninsula without talking about mining. It played a major role in the U.P.'s economic development in the last half of the nineteenth century and the first half of the twentieth. And there are indications now, with new technology and greater demand, that mining may return to the U.P. in full force.

Ever wonder what it was like to go to work, lunch bag in hand, in a dark, dug-out cave that was hundreds of feet underground? And not come up for fresh air and sunlight for ten or twelve hours?

Stop by the Delaware Mine, just south of Copper Harbor, and you can walk, unescorted, down the steps into the mine, then traverse 1400 feet through the mine which features informative signs along the way.

It's cold down there, forty-five degrees, so bring a jacket. Dogs are welcome but some might balk at the cold and darkness.

You'll get a good sense of what a lovely job this was between 1847 and 1887 when the mine was operating. All you needed was a sledgehammer to dig out the copper.

Wages? A whopping fourteen to twenty-one cents an hour.

The Delaware Mine isn't as elaborate as a few of the other historic mines in the U.P., but it's inexpensive, and some people prefer the self-guided tours.

You'll spend about an hour here, and one of the highlights is above ground in the gift shop: two tame, de-scented pet skunks who will gladly eat a treat from your hand and maybe consent to a photograph with you.

The mine is open June through October.

Phone: 906-289-4688

Directions: Drive twelve miles south of Copper Harbor on US-41.

Keweenaw Autumn Drive

Autumn in the Upper Peninsula is stupendous, and there's probably no better place to enjoy the color change than in the Keweenaw Peninsula. If you're looking for a commanding vista, go to Brockway Mountain outside of Copper Harbor, but you'd be hard-pressed to find a more awe-inspiring sight in fall than the last ten miles into Copper Harbor on US-41.

It looks like the gateway to heaven.

Here's what you'll see: a winding, ten mile tunnel of gold, yellow, red and green. The trees cross over the two lane highway creating a wondrous canopy.

The speed limit is forty five miles per hour; you'll want to go fifteen.

You'll find a few places on the road where you can turn out to take pictures. The Keweenaw Mountain Lodge, just south of Copper Harbor, is the only commercial establishment on the ten mile stretch.

Best time to go? Late September, early October. The peak, barring a major wind storm, lasts about two weeks.

The good news for leaf-lovers is once you finish driving through this gateway to heaven, you can actually go to heaven because the entrance to Brockway Mountain is just about a mile away.

Directions: Drive north on US-41 toward Copper Harbor

Brockway Mountain Drive

This steep, winding nine mile drive between Copper Harbor and Eagle Harbor is one of the most scenic stretches of road in the United States. If you're driving a stick-shift, you'll be down-shifting to second gear much of the time. If you're driving a motorcycle, keep your eye on the road and not the awe-inspiring scenery. If you're on a bicycle, well, good luck.

Brockway Mountain Drive rises more than 700 feet above Lake Superior and gives you commanding views of the big lake, along with Copper Harbor, Eagle Harbor, Lake Medora, the surrounding hills and forests, and on a good, clear day, even Isle Royale fifty miles away.

You can stop at plenty of vistas along the way. There's a small gift shop at the top of the mountain.

No speed limit signs. You won't need them.

The road was built back in 1933 with federal funds during the Depression. Parts of the road, especially in the northern section near Copper Harbor, feel like they haven't been repaired since the Thirties.

Just consider that part of Brockway's charm.

It's a great place to star-gaze. Also ideal for spotting hawks migrating in April, wildflowers blooming in June, and the leaves changing in September and October.

Brockway Mountain Drive is closed in the winter. Bring your snowmobile, instead. And for you adventurous snowshoers? What, are you nuts?

Directions: Drive just west of Copper Harbor on M-26, turn at sign to Brockway Mountain.

12
Copper Harbor

If you start on US-41 in Miami, Florida, and drive 1990 miles north, you'll end up in Copper Harbor. It's the end of the line. Drive any farther, and you'll find yourself in Lake Superior.

If you're looking for bustling streets and an exciting night life, you've come to the wrong place.

There's no downtown here. Instead, it's just a random assortment of galleries, book stores, gift shops, restaurants and motels interspersed among empty blocks and fields. You'll be doing a fair amount of walking or bike riding here.

Hiking and biking trails abound. The views of the harbor are gorgeous.

Copper Harbor was just that–a harbor for copper shipments–back in the nineteenth century, but it's been a quaint, sleepy community with an affinity for recreation and the arts ever since. If you have blood pressure problems, this town will provide therapy for you.

It also features a surprisingly good restaurant, the Harbor House, and the launching spot for a ferry to Isle Royale.

Some tourists have wondered why Copper Harbor, with all its charms, isn't more crowded. A merchant explains why: "Because that's the way we like it."

Website: www.copperharbor.org/

Directions: Drive north on US-41 until you can't go any farther.

Gay

This is a town with a distinctive name, a distinctive feature and a distinctive bar.

First, the name. It comes from the town's founder Joseph Gay and has absolutely nothing to do with "gays." Sorry. That would have made it so much more newsworthy.

Now, the feature. Acres upon acres of stamp sands which are the residue from a copper processing plant after the copper has been pounded or "stamped."

The grayish, gravelly sand from the Mohawk Mining Company piled up year after year to a point where it forms a rolling prairie that nestles up next to Lake Superior. It's a strange, almost surreal sight that would have driven environmentalists crazy had environmentalists been around when the mining company was operating between 1898 and 1933.

A sign at the entrance to the stamp sands warns you not to take any of the stamp sands away. Seriously, who's just dying to bring some stamp sands home with them?

And finally, the bar. Yes, it's called The Gay Bar, just down the road from the stamp sands. The menus are pink and you can buy risqué souvenirs that play up the name, but walk inside and you won't hear any pounding dance music nor will you want to order a cosmo.

Instead, you'll find a friendly, down-home bar that offers twenty-seven types of hot dogs, with chips, for about five bucks.

Before you leave, make sure you pose next to the big Gay Bar sign outside. You'll be about the ten millionth customer, gay and straight, to do so.

Phone: 906-296-0951

Website: www.thegaybar.com/

Address: 925 Lake Street, Gay

Alberta Village Museum

The story goes like this: Henry Ford was motoring across the U.P. one afternoon with his friends Thomas Edison and Harvey Firestone when they stopped outside of L'Anse for lunch, and Ford, who owned 750,000 acres in the U.P., declared that this would be a fine spot for a sawmill and an industrial village.

So he built the mill and founded the town of Alberta, which he named after the daughter of one of his executives. Rich and powerful people can do such things.

The sawmill was built in 1935 to produce wood for the early Ford cars and later for the "woodies."

What you see here today is the sawmill exactly as it existed back in the Thirties, along with a little village of twelve houses for the workers, and two tiny school houses.

Ford's vision was to make this an entirely self-sustaining community, producing its own energy and growing its own crops. He never quite achieved that because, honestly, who wants a car even partially made out of wood?

Ford's son donated Alberta and the sawmill to Michigan Tech in 1954. It's now used as a conference center, but you can stop by from June to October, Monday through Thursday, 10 a.m. to 5 p.m., and get a sense of what it was like to work and live here in the middle of nowhere in what was truly a "planned community."

Fans of Henry Ford, of automobiles and of American history will love it here. Others? Maybe not so much.

One more thing: the last saw operator at the mill is now making exquisite birdseye maple furniture on site. Take a look at the $16,000 rocking chair he built. It'd be a swell addition to your front porch.

Phone: 906-524-6181

Directions: Drive nine miles south of L'Anse on US-41.

Photos by Elizabeth Peterson

Lucy Hill Luge

Have you ever wondered what it's like to come barreling down a slope of solid ice on a skinny, little sled, with your head and shoulders hanging precariously over the edge? Well, that pretty much describes what it's like to be a luger.

And if you're looking for that Olympic kind of experience, you can do it at Lucy Hill in Negaunee.

The cost? Free, if you get there on Friday evenings in the winter, and that includes the sled, special spiked shoes, a helmet and instruction. Go there on Saturday afternoons, and they'll charge you ten dollars to ride as many times as you like.

Lucy Hill is unique in the United States. It's a natural, not artificial, luge run. No fiberglass siding here. If you run off the ice, you plow into a snow bank, wooden rails, or hay bales. You don't get hurt, the staff makes sure of that, but you will have to sign a waiver before you take to the ice.

They start beginners at the bottom of the run where you don't have to turn; you just have to slide and keep your wits about yourself. They'll move you up the run as you show progress in your steering abilities.

Lugers here have ranged from three years old to seventy-five.

The Upper Peninsula Luge Club, which sponsors an after-school program here, runs the facility.

Website: www.negauneeluge.freehomepage.com

Address: 230 E. County Road, Negaunee

Directions: From US-41, turn south on Teal Lake Avenue, then right on West Main Street, then left on Pioneer Avenue, then left on East County Road, stay right to the luge track.

16

Negaunee Antiquing

Antiquing isn't for everybody but if it's your thing, head to Negaunee where you'll find four shops located on the same block of Iron Street downtown. Two of them are huge. You could spend an entire afternoon here and still not see everything.

Jewelry, dishes, silverware, paintings, books, furniture, candleholders–you'll find them all here. Vinyl records? They got them. Old time cash registers? Yep. Wooden snow shoes? You'll find a pair to fit you.

And if you want to take a break during your shopping adventures, stop at the Midtown Bakery on the same block for coffee, a sandwich or a bowl of soup. It offers up homemade food, friendly service and a quaint, down-home atmosphere.

A few further words about antiquing at these four shops (The Old Bank Building, Lowensteins, Adora's Antiques, and Tickled Pink). First, don't expect Iron Street to be cute and precious. It's not. The buildings are mostly late nineteenth and early twentieth century architecture but, frankly, they're kind of homely. A few even look decrepit.

Second…and here's the good news: the prices of the items inside are more than reasonable. Some are downright cheap, and a smart antiquer will walk out of here with a trunkload of merchandise without having to take out a second mortgage on her house.

Directions: From US-41, turn south on North Teal Lake Road, then right on West Main Street, then left on North Pioneer Avenue, then quick right on Iron Street. Shops are a couple of blocks down.

Little Presque Isle

This is more than a beach. It's actually an expedition. Bring good shoes that you can wear in the water.

Okay, now the explanation: Little Presque Isle is an island located about one hundred yards away from a beautiful, sandy beach about fifteen minutes northwest of Marquette. The beach is fine and the water's about as warm as any you'll find on Lake Superior, but the real fun comes in making the trek, across a mostly rocky bottom, from the beach to the island.

It's an adventure. Kids will love it but hold on to the little ones. The deepest the water ever gets is only about two feet, but the footing can be slippery and waves will occasionally slap at you.

More fun awaits on the island. Hike around it, picnic on it, even jump off the cliffs if you dare. Watch for where the locals do it. You could spend a day here easily.

Camping is discouraged, but it's not unusual to see tents out here.

Needless to say, Little Presque Isle is not a place to take Grandpa with his arthritic hips. Even getting from the parking lot through the pine forest to the beach is a quarter mile walk. There are plenty of much more accessible beaches in the U.P.

But if you're healthy and adventurous and you don't mind getting wet, you've found the perfect spot.

Rover's welcome, as well.

Directions: Drive about seven miles north on County Road 550 (Big Bay Road) from Marquette. Watch for the small sign on the right to Little Presque Isle.

Sugarloaf Mountain

Are you looking for a little adventure, some moderate exercise, and gorgeous views? You couldn't do much better than Sugarloaf Mountain, six miles north of Marquette. Just head north on County Road 550 (the road to Big Bay) and you'll see the sign for Sugarloaf and a parking lot there on the right.

Get out of the vehicle and start climbing. You'll have the choice of taking the quicker but steeper path, or the easier one. Kids, grandparents and first-timers would probably prefer the easier route. All told, your journey to the top of the 1000 foot high mountain will take about a half hour, but there are plenty of places to rest along the way.

Enjoy the climb, the tall trees, the rock formations, the startlingly fresh air and the occasional wildlife as you make your way up.

On the top of Sugarloaf is a large viewing deck. To the north and east are breathtaking views of Lake Superior; to the south is Marquette, and to the west are forests and mountains.

If you're warmly bundled up, wintertime climbs are wonderful. Any time of year, the views are most spectacular at dawn and dusk, especially if there's only limited cloud cover.

A suggestion? If it's warm enough and not too windy, take a picnic with you. You'll feel like you're feasting on top of the world.

Directions: Drive about five miles north on CR 550 from Marquette. The sign for Sugarloaf Mountain on the right is large. You can't miss it.

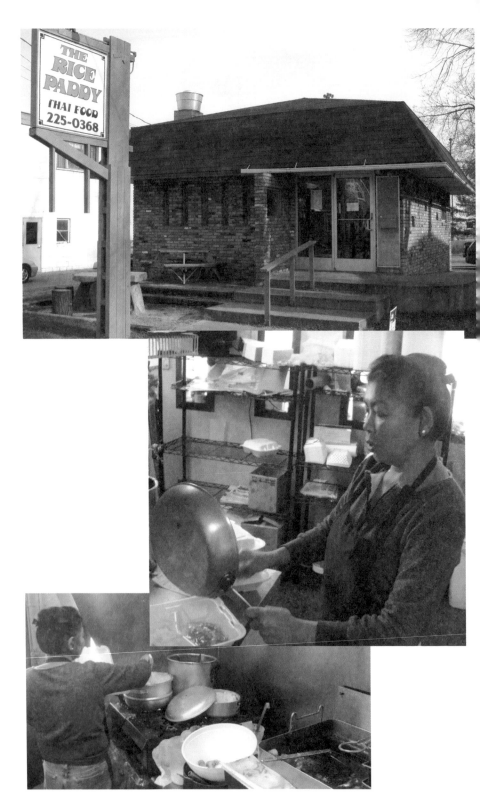

19

Rice Paddy

This place has become a legend in Marquette. It's a one-woman operation that specializes in low-priced Thai and Chinese food. It's mostly takeout, but there is seating for about ten people inside, and in warmer weather, you can sit outside on a couple of picnic tables.

The food is authentic, satisfying and delicious, but the co-attraction is Aoy (OY), the Thai-American owner and chef. She's there six days a week (not Saturdays), mixing and stirring, dipping and frying, spicing and slicing, all the while dispensing playful insults to her customers and greeting everybody who walks through the door with, "What you want, boyfriend?" or "What you want, girlfriend?"

Don't expect fast food; she'll likely tell you to come back in forty-five minutes because she's always busy, and she cooks every meal fresh and individually.

She's not politically correct and she'll occasionally utter a few curse words but she's lovable. Just ask NMU students, doctors, lawyers and everybody else. She'll cook free meals for people in need, and once a year, she takes the money from her tip jar on the counter to buy shoes and school supplies for impoverished children back in her homeland.

Aoy's got a big heart, she'll entertain you with her conversation and she'll serve you great food.

You can get a snack here for a few dollars, or splurge on a hearty meal for seven dollars. Insults are free.

Address: 1720 Presque Isle Avenue, Marquette

Phone: 906-225-0368

Web: www.eatricepaddy.com/

Northstar Lounge

If you're looking for the perfect spot for an intimate conversation over drinks or a meal–with a sensational view–you can't do any better than the Northstar Lounge on top of the Landmark Inn in Marquette.

On one side, you're looking out over the Eastside neighborhood, complete with graceful churches and century-old homes; on the other side, you've got a commanding view of Lake Superior.

In the summertime, it's light outside until 10:30 p.m and you'll see sailboats gracefully gliding back toward the harbor. In the winter, darkness descends at 5 p.m. and the lights flicker on. At Christmastime, the neighborhood view takes on the look of a Dickens village.

There's a gas fireplace in the corner of the lounge that warms the place up.

The Northstar isn't all that big so sometimes you might have to wait to get a seat. It's worth the wait.

Beer might cost you four or five dollars, wine a little more. Or just order coffee and a dessert.

It's a great way to wrap up an evening and engage in a little seduction–romantic, business or otherwise.

Address: 230 North Front Street (sixth floor of Landmark Inn),
Marquette

Phone: 906-228-2580

Web: www.thelandmarkinn.com/

Photos by UP200

UP 200

The UP 200 in mid-February is one of those rare sled dog races that actually starts in the middle of a town in front of a large crowd. The dogs line up on Washington Street in downtown Marquette where the spectators are packed two and three deep, cheering as the twelve-dog teams and their mushers take off on their 250 mile journey through the cold, snow and ice of the Upper Peninsula.

Temperatures at start time, usually around 7 p.m., range from zero to thirty degrees, and winds, on occasion, have been fierce.

But that's all part of the experience. Just dress up in layers, put on some heavy gloves and a hat that covers your ears, and you're all set.

If you get cold, take cover in Babycakes coffee shop for a few minutes, and grab some coffee or hot chocolate.

But the attraction here is the dogs, most of them Alaskan huskies. You might be surprised because these dogs aren't the classic, broad-shouldered breed. Instead, they're lean and athletic, bred for long distance running. And they're noisy and raring to go.

Get there early and you'll be able to pet some of the dogs and talk to the mushers about racing strategy.

The cost? Nothing except for the coffee or hot chocolate.

Address: Downtown Washington Street, Marquette

Web: www.up200.org/

Marquette Regional History Center

Let's be honest. Most small town history museums look kind of like glorified garage sales, right? They've got a black-and-white photo of the town's founder in the front, a musket on the side table, a rusty Olivetti typewriter in the back, some old-timey kitchen utensils on the counter in the corner, and a stained hoop skirt hanging from the wall.

It's all cute and charming but…

The Marquette Regional History Center, remarkably, does not have a small town feel to it.

First of all, there's five million dollars invested here in a beautiful, graceful building, inside and out.

Second, a half million pieces have been donated to the museum, only a fraction of which you can see at one time.

And third, you actually learn something here–about the geological and marine history of the Upper Peninsula, the wildlife, the Indians and pioneers, the settlers and farmers.

Along the way, you'll gaze in at an actual Ojibwe wigwam and at a birch bark canoe.

You'll see one of the first-ever snowmobiles and a baby carriage that converts to a sleigh. Yooper stuff.

But the place is classy. It's kind of a mini-Smithsonian in the middle of the U.P.

Admission for adults is seven dollars, seniors six, students three, and kids twelve and under cost two bucks.

Address: 145 West Spring Street, Marquette

Phone: 906-226-3571

Web: www.marquettecohistory.org/

Upper Peninsula Children's Museum

All right, so you've come to Marquette with your children for a visit, and all of the sudden it starts raining. Or snowing. The kids, all set to hit the beach or the bike paths or the mountain trails, gloomily look out the window and inform you that they're bored.

Here's what you do. Head to the Upper Peninsula Children's Museum downtown, and it's almost guaranteed that once they climb the steps to the museum, their eyes will open wide, they'll let out a screech of excitement, and they'll be off on a journey of discovery for two or three hours.

Along the way, they may find a playmate in a pet boa or python. Yes, the snakes do come out of their cages. They'll feed turtles and tortoises, they'll climb into the cockpit of a jet, they'll practice anchoring on a TV news set, they'll operate a control room at a radio station, they'll run an elaborate model train in a mining village.

Hours of fun, and kids may not realize it but they're learning stuff here, too.

One caveat: The age range here is about two to ten years old. Bring a pre-teen or a teenager into the museum, and she's likely to take a bleary, bored look at the exhibits, and say to you, "Seriously?"

Admission? Five dollars for adults and children. Kids under two are free.

Address: 123 West Baraga Avenue, Marquette

Phone: 906-226-3911

Web: www.upchildrensmuseum.com/

24

Marquette Farmers Market

Do you sometimes wish that we could turn back the clock in America, and get away from enormous, impersonal shopping malls, congested highways and a lifestyle that's dominated by technology?

You're not alone.

Stop by the Marquette Farmers Market on Saturdays, 9 a.m. to 2 p.m., from May through October, and you'll get some much needed therapy.

Time slows down. People actually talk to each other and smile. Almost no one's on a cell phone. The produce and meat you buy are fresh and local. The breads just came out of the oven. The flowers were just picked. The jewelry, candles, and walking canes were crafted by local artists and artisans.

How about a local Bloody Mary mix? They got that, too, perfect for a Saturday morning hangover.

Farmers Markets are springing up all over, but this is one of the very best, with more than forty vendors at a wonderful downtown location at the Commons.

Dogs are now discouraged but everybody else is welcome. You don't have to spend a cent if you don't want to, but you might want to consider forking out a few bucks for a cup of coffee and a muffin, sitting down under a bright, sunny sky, and enjoying the musicians while the crowds of contented shoppers slowly make their way, booth by booth, around the market.

Now, if you're partial to indoor mega-malls with piped in, easy listening music, trendy chain stores, and hordes of teenagers yakking on their cell phones, you'll need to head south, out of the U.P.

Address: 112 South Third Street (The Commons), Marquette

Phone: 906-228-9475

Web: www.mqtfarmersmarket.com/

25

Lakenenland

This is a truly one-of-a-kind place.

It's nearly forty acres of junkyard art, the whimsical, playful, fantastical creations of ironworker Tommy Lakenen.

Lakenen used to display these sculptures at home but he ran afoul of the local planning and zoning boards, so he decided to buy this plot of land off of M-28, fifteen miles east of Marquette, to display his art.

And it *is* art, most of it representational, some of it abstract, much of it with a message. You'll see Lakenen's version of lumberjacks, a snowmobile, a stunt motorcyclist, mermaids, an alligator, hockey players. The list goes on and on, and it's growing. Lakenen is prolific.

You can see the eighty-plus sculptures in a quarter mile circuit around the property, either by walking or driving. Many of the sculptures invite you to get out and interact with them.

And there's more at Lakenenland, including a bandshell for concerts, a playground, and a fishing pond. You didn't bring a fishing pole? Don't worry, Lakenen has left some there to borrow. Free.

Drop by in the winter and you may find a bonfire warming visitors who've stopped by for some steaming hot chocolate and hearty companionship. Snowmobilers love the place.

It's open twenty-four hours a day, 365 days a year.

It's free. Donations are accepted but not expected.

What a deal.

Some visitors might consider Lakenenland wacky and odd. Others will see it as a delightful fusion of art, fun and a sense of community. They're right.

It's Yooperism at its finest.

Directions: Drive about fifteen miles east of Marquette on M-28. Look for the big sculpture and the sign on the right.

Web: www.lakenenland.com/

Eben Ice Caves

This is one of the Upper Peninsula's natural wonders during wintertime. If you happen by here during the warmer months, what you'll see is a modest, little creek trickling thirty feet over a limestone and shale cliff into a creek bed below. Nothing special.

In the winter, though, the water freezes as it descends and transforms itself into gorgeous columns of ice. The rock wall curves inward so that you can actually walk between the wall and the translucent formations of ice.

If you're planning to visit, though, prepare for a trek. You'll be walking more than a mile on snow across a field and through a magnificent maple tree forest. If the path is packed down and it usually is because the Ice Caves are a popular site, boots are fine. Many hikers, however, bring their snowshoes which allow them to venture off the trail.

The last couple hundred yards can be a little treacherous. You might slip and fall a few times, but don't worry. It's just snow. Great fun for the whole family but kids under seven and the elderly may struggle with it. Dress warmly.

Rover's welcome as long as you think he can handle up to two hours in the snow.

Directions: Drive south on US-41 out of Marquette. After seventeen miles, turn left (east) on M-94. Drive twelve miles until you get to Eben and the New Moon bar. Take a left there and drive one and a half miles until you get to Frey Road. Take a right there until you come to a curve in the road. Park there. You'll probably see other cars and other people starting their trek to the caves.

Trenary Outhouse Classic

You might consider this the U.P.'s scaled-down version of Mardi Gras. Except for the fact that 1) it's in tiny Trenary instead of New Orleans 2) there's snow on the ground, and 3) Yoopers celebrate with outhouses instead of elaborate floats.

Otherwise, they're almost identical.

It happens the last Saturday in February in this community where the population swells from a few hundred to 4000 for the races. It can get rowdy but it's a lot of fun.

Here's how it works: the contestants–men, women and children– construct outhouses, complete with toilets and toilet paper, then mount them on skis, and then race the contraptions 500 feet down Trenary's main street.

Some of the outhouses are remarkably creative, some are funny, others are a tad vulgar, and a few are just built for speed.

But here's the thing. It doesn't really matter who wins. The outhouse races, like so many events in the U.P., are just a wonderful excuse for friends and strangers to get together and drink, eat, laugh and have fun. If you're looking for an outdoor party in the middle of winter, it doesn't get much better than this. Dress warmly.

Rover's welcome on a leash.

Web: www.trenaryouthouseclassic.com/

Directions: From Marquette, drive 33 miles south on US-41. Take a left on M-67N. Drive a half mile and you're there.

Falling Rock Cafe

If you're partial to Starbucks, you'll find two of them in the U.P. and they're both in Marquette.

However, if you long for something a little different, more Yooperlike, try the Falling Rock Café in Munising.

What you'll find is a huge café, in a century-old building, with scuffed and sloping birdseye maple floors, decorative yellow tin on the walls, and mismatched chairs and tables.

And 50,000 used and new books on the shelves. And WiFi.

The place is comfortable and welcoming. The coffee, sandwiches, soups and ice cream are delicious.

Stop in, order a latte from a decidedly unpretentious barista, select a couple of books from the shelves to peruse and maybe buy, sit down on one of the mismatched chairs, and soak in the atmosphere.

While you're there, you might observe a club meeting or class of some sort, a jam session, a lecture, a book-signing or who-knows-what.

The Falling Rock, the brainchild of two academics who left Florida several years ago for a more satisfying life up north, serves as the de facto community center of Munising.

It's not going to win any awards for architecture and furnishings, but it can easily win your heart.

Address: 104 East Munising Avenue, Munising

Phone: 906-387-3008

Web: www.fallingrockcafe.com/

Miners Castle, Falls & Beach

Drive eleven miles east of Munising and you'll find one of the most remarkable sandstone formations in the United States. Miners Castle, overlooking Lake Superior, was formed 500 million years ago.

Over the years, it's been beaten up by the harsh weather; in fact, in 2006, two of its so-called turrets broke off and plunged into the lake below.

Savor the sight, enjoy some of the trails around it, and take photos to impress the folks back home.

Just a few miles up the road, don your walking shoes for a half mile hike deep into a hardwood forest. At the end, you'll find Miners Falls, fifty feet high, tucked away amid the greenery, atop another sandstone formation. Beautiful.

Then, two minutes down the road, park the car and take the family to Miners Beach. A boardwalk, through a pine forest with picnic tables and barbecue grills, directs you down to a spectacular white sand beach alongside the cliffs of Pictured Rocks. Grand Island beckons in the distance beyond the blue-green waters of Lake Superior. You could spend hours here.

No dogs allowed. Leave Rover in a shaded car with a bowl of water, or better yet, leave him at home.

Web: www.nps.gov/piro/index.htm

Phone: 906-387-3700

Directions: Head east on H-58 out of Munising. After five miles, take a left (north) on Miners Castle Road. Drive five miles until you can't go any farther.

Sable Falls & Grand Sable Dunes

Here are two distinctly different adventures, right next door to each other. You'll find Sable Falls and Grand Sable Dunes just over a mile west of Grand Marais.

From the parking lot, take a right toward the falls and you'll notice, almost immediately as you descend into the dense forest toward the falls, that the temperature drops sharply. Ten degrees or more. It's refreshing on a summer day.

The falls are a series of cascades, rather than one large one, but they're remarkably picturesque. Enjoy the fifteen minute hike downhill because it's easy, and where do you end up? On the beach. Spectacular.

Take a rest there, in the shadow of an enormous dune, before heading back. The hike upstream, especially if Junior's whining or Grandpa's arthritic hip is acting up, might take closer to a half hour.

Then venture out to the top of the dunes. It's another invigorating hike that might take ten minutes, or twenty, depending on how far you choose to go and how badly you get bogged down in the sand. The dunes rise almost 300 feet above Lake Superior.

What you'll notice as you walk is the forest slowly giving way to the sand. They're two conflicting forces of nature, and experts say the sand will always win. It'll cover the trees and bury them eventually.

Take your time on this walk, especially in the heat of the summer. Bring water. Don't let the sand bury you.

Rover's not allowed at the dunes or the falls.

Web: www.nps.gov/piro/planyourvisit/waterfalls.htm

www.nps.gov/piro/planyourvisit/scenicsites.htm

Phone: 906-387-3700

Directions: Drive one mile west of Grand Marais on H-58.

Tahquamenon Falls

This is on every tourist's to-do list when they visit the Upper Peninsula, but don't let that deter you. The falls truly are beautiful.

They're actually two sets of falls. The Upper Falls are spectacular, fifty feet high and 200 feet across; they're the third largest waterfall east of the Mississippi River. They cascade over sandstone that's 500 million years old. You can reach the overview after an easy five minute walk, but if you're more adventurous, you can descend the steps toward the brink of the falls. Be forewarned, you'll be huffing and puffing by the time you reach the top of the stairs on your way back.

To reach the Lower Falls of the Tahquamenon River, you can either drive down the road about five minutes, or you can pack your water jug and hike the trail four miles along the river.

The Lower Falls are actually five distinct, smaller cascades, less dramatic but equally scenic. You can rent boats here and paddle around.

Rover, on a leash, is welcome at Tahquamenon Falls. If he's a water dog, keep your eye on him, though. The Upper Falls (50,000 gallons of water crashing down each second) is no place for a playful romp.

You can also visit the falls in the winter. Snowmobile trails are close by.

A Recreation Passport is required.

One other hint: The Upper Falls boasts a great brewery and pub. Drink your beer *after* you visited the falls.

Phone: 906-492-3415

Directions: From Newberry, take M-123 north for 25 miles to the Lower Falls, 29 miles to the Upper Falls.

32

Point Iroquois Lighthouse

Lighthouses are like waterfalls in the Upper Peninsula; there are plenty of them, and you can't go wrong visiting any of them.

The Point Iroquois Lighthouse, however, is one of the most important. It was first built out of wood in 1857 to help direct ships toward the newly constructed Soo Locks, just seventeen miles away, but then rebuilt in 1870 out of brick. That structure stands there today, perched on the western end of the St. Mary's River.

You can climb the narrow, winding, five story staircase to the top of the lighthouse where you get a commanding view of the lake and Canada just five miles away.

But what the Point Iroquois Lighthouse gives you, more than anything else, is an appreciation for what it was like to be a lighthouse keeper back in the nineteenth century.

You'll find old photos and displays here, along with a lighthouse light, a lens, a ship's compass, a radio direction finder, even one of the original uniforms of a lighthouse keeper. Who knew they wore uniforms?

An especially affecting exhibit is the restored living quarters of the keeper's family in the lighthouse, complete with a garment on the ironing board, a cinnamon bun cooling on the kitchen table, and a checkers game, half-played, in the living room. It's kind of eerie.

It's a great place to visit, but living here in isolation as the lighthouse keepers and their families did–with few roads, virtually no neighbors, no stores, and no TV? It's not a life most of us would choose.

But they played a vital role in the history of the Great Lakes, and heck, the job was lucrative. The lighthouse keeper made 600 bucks a year.

The lighthouse is open from Memorial Day through October 15.

Address: 12942 West Lakeshore Drive, Brimley Phone: 906-437-5272

Directions: Drive six miles west of Brimley on West Lakeshore Drive.

33

Dancing Crane Coffee House

This ain't a fancy, cosmopolitan espresso house.

But it is an oasis for good coffee from Sumatra, Honduras, Peru, Uganda, and Ethiopia. Folgers? Not so much.

The coffee house was built in 2006 by the LeBlanc family in the Bay Mills Indian Community, a few miles north of Brimley. The structure is chinked logs and filled with charm.

You'll find coffee (cheap!) lovingly roasted and brewed here, along with fourteen types of smoothies, teas, soups, ice cream, and brats and burgers grilled on the porch.

Native American arts and crafts are on display and for sale.

How about a genuine, operating Pac Man machine? Yep. It'll cost you a quarter to play.

The real treat, though, is the LeBlanc family who operate the coffee house with a sense of obligation to provide a healthful, welcoming, friendly gathering place for the community. With great coffee.

Locals make up most of the clientele, but downstaters and other tourists frequently make their way up here. So far, visitors from sixty-four countries have stopped in to savor a cup of java at the Dancing Crane.

A great place, all year round, to see what a coffee house is supposed to be: a casual, comfortable place to talk with old friends and meet new ones.

Address: 12072 West Lakeshore Drive, Brimley

Phone: 906-248-3387

Directions: Drive about five miles west of Brimley on West Lakeshore Drive. The coffee house is on the right.

Soo Locks

One of the favorite tourist stops in the Upper Peninsula, and it doesn't cost a dime.

Every year, 10,000 ships pass through the locks which connect Lake Superior to Lake Huron and the lower Great Lakes. If you're a fan of maritime history and commerce, or you just think big ships and barges are really cool, you've got to stop here and take a look.

You'll climb the stairs to a viewing deck alongside the locks.

One caveat, however: What you'll witness is not especially dramatic and exciting. The vessel pulls into the lock chamber, the gate closes, and then the water level is either slowly raised or lowered because Lake Superior is twenty-one feet higher in elevation than Lake Huron. Then the other gate opens, and the vessel moves on.

Slowly. It all takes about a half hour.

Junior, unless he's a budding engineer, might be getting restless after fifteen minutes.

Informative exhibits and a film inside the Visitors Center answer all your questions about the locks.

The locks are closed from January 15th to March 25th because, of course, the lakes ice up. The Visitors Center is open from May 15th to October 15th.

Address: 312 West Portage Avenue, Sault Ste. Marie

Phone: 906-632-7020 (Visitors Center)

Great Lakes Boat Building School

This is one of only five boat building schools in the entire country and visitors are welcome at any time to come by and watch the students lovingly craft their wooden boats.

It's heartening to see craftsmanship and a traditional material, like wood, come back into vogue. Wooden boats saw a resurgence of interest start in the 1970s and it's continued ever since. Every student who's graduated here, in either a one or two year course, has been able to find a job in the industry.

Cedarville is the ideal spot for the school; this is the gateway to the Les Cheneaux Islands which are a mecca for boaters and fishermen.

If you're a wooden boating enthusiast or have an interest in this nation's maritime history or you just like to watch people make pretty things, schedule some time here. The students and instructors will be glad to put down their tools for a few minutes and talk to you about their craft. They love what they do. How many of us can say that?

You can also take a picnic lunch, walk around back, and sit down for a meal on scenic Cedarville Bay. And wonder about your own choice of career. Maybe you'd rather be crafting beautiful wooden boats instead of pounding on your damn keyboard in your cramped cubicle, back in your congested, crime-ridden city.

Address: 485 South Meridian Road, Cedarville

Phone: 906-484-1081

Web: www.glbbs.org/

36

Hessel Marina

Hessel is a tidy, scenic, little village on the coast of Lake Huron where time slows down a bit.

Suggestion: Order a sandwich or a hot dog out of the Hessel Grocery and Deli across from the marina, then cross the street for a leisurely lunch while you watch the boats cruise in and out of the harbor.

The Les Cheneaux Islands, famous for boating and fishing, lie just a mile or two away.

This is a village that was originally home to Native American fishermen, then became a busy lumber port, and now has become a quaint, sleepy, and altogether appealing destination for boaters, fishermen, and vacationers who are looking to escape the hustle and bustle of the cities and suburbs.

It's a great place to charter a boat or venture out on an eco-tour, but if you're just looking for a quiet, scenic, inexpensive respite on your journey through the U.P., you could do a lot worse than enjoying a bag lunch under the sun at the Hessel Marina.

Wintertime? Well, you might want to order soup, instead, and cover yourself with four layers of clothing.

Address: 197 Pickford Avenue, Hessel (Hessel Grocery and Deli). The marina is across the street.

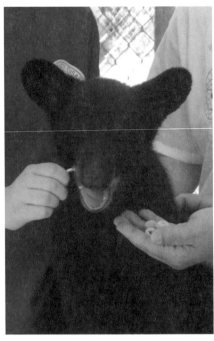

Oswald's Bear Ranch

All right, this one isn't free. It's twenty dollars for a carful of people so if you can cram six people into your vehicle, that's less than four dollars apiece. Individually, it's ten dollars a person. If you got it, spend it.

You'll be able to see, at last count, twenty-nine bears up close, in a natural habitat spread over eighty acres. They're behind fences, of course, shading themselves, dozing off, and occasionally wandering over to entertain the gaping homo sapiens.

The bears range from a few months to twenty years old.

And here's the thing. These are all rescue bears who, if they hadn't come here, likely would have died or been killed or sent to a zoo. Oswald's Bear Ranch gives them a much better life and allows folks like us to get a better sense of how they live. Hint: they're cute and active when they're young, and big and sluggish when they get older.

They're separated by age and gender (no mating allowed) and you can visit them by walking a trail around the various, large, fenced habitats. If you're old or infirm, you can hitch a ride in a cart for a five dollar donation.

You want a close up photo with you nestling a hopelessly cute cub? Another five bucks.

But understand, running a bear farm costs money. Dean Oswald started the place because he loves bears. He considers them his kids. He just needs a little help from the rest of us to help raise his family.

Oswald's Bear Ranch is open from the Friday before Memorial Day through September.

Address: 13814 County Road 407, Newberry Phone: 906-293-3147

Web: www.oswaldsbearranch.com/

Directions: From Newberry, drive four miles north on M-123, then take a left (west) at County Road 407, and go four and a half miles.

Chamberlin's Ole Forest Inn

This is a place where, on a cold winter's evening, you walk inside and glance at the fire crackling in the huge stone fireplace, and you say, "Aaaaahhhhh…"

You shed your coat, plop down in one of the overstuffed chairs next to the fireplace, order a drink, and then realize that life doesn't get much better than this.

That's winter, when the snowmobilers and cross-country skiers come here for rest, relaxation and warmth. Now, in the summer, the crowds are bigger and they're sprawled on comfortable chairs spread all over the wraparound porch and the huge lawn, gazing out at majestic Big Manistique Lake.

Yeah, life's pretty damn good then, too.

Chamberlin's is a bed-and-breakfast, in a building that dates back to the late nineteenth century, but it's also a cozy restaurant and bar, and it plays host to several events in the charming, little town of Curtis.

Here, surrounded by lakes, forests and fields, you can get away from it all, for a few hours or a few days, and just say, "Aaaaahhh…"

Chamberlin's is closed in April.

Address: N9450 Manistique Lakes Road, Curtis (aka Highway 33)

Phone: 906-586-6000

Web: www.chamberlinsinn.com/

Seney National Wildlife Refuge

If you like nonstop thrills, this is not the place for you. If you're a big fan of zoos, where you're guaranteed to see the tiger in the cage over here, the elephant over there, and the gorilla in the back corner, then Seney is probably not going to be your cup of tea, either.

However, if you like the idea of discovering wildlife in their natural homes, spread out over a 96,000 acre refuge, then this is the place for you. Are you a bird watcher? You can't miss this.

You need patience here, and you'll be rewarded. Loons, swans, osprey, sand hill cranes, bald eagles, beaver, deer, river otters, black bears, coyotes, turtles–they and many others are all out in the marshes, ponds and forests on the refuge. You just have to slow down, maybe sit down, and wait for the animals to show themselves.

Two ways to view the wildlife: 1) On a 1.4 mile walk around the ponds and marshes, just behind the Visitors Center, and 2) On a seven mile drive through the refuge where the speed limit is fifteen miles per hour. You'll probably find yourself stopping several times.

There's a good chance you'll see dozens of swans and loons along the way.

The cost? Nothing, but donations would be nice. No pressure.

The Visitor Center and the seven mile drive are open from May 15th to October 15th. The staff here is very friendly and well-informed.

Rover is welcome, on a leash.

Bugs, unfortunately, are also welcome.

Phone: 906-586-9851

Web: www.fws.gov/midwest/seney/ (US Fish and Wildlife Service)

Directions: Drive six miles south of Seney on M-77.

Photo By Chelsea Cabell

Kitch-iti-kipi

This is a sight to behold. Kitch-iti-kipi, which means "big, cold water," is the largest freshwater spring in Michigan, but that description doesn't do it much justice.

It's a body of water, 300 feet by 175 feet and forty feet deep, that has an almost surreal, emerald hue. And it's crystal clear, allowing you to spot something as tiny as a quarter at the bottom, forty feet down. Amazing.

But what really makes this spring special is that you can cross it in a large, sturdy, self-operated boat. You, or better yet, one of your kids, turns a large wheel that's attached to a cable, and that propels you slowly across the spring.

Look down into the clear, crystalline water and you'll see lake trout, brown trout and an occasional yellow perch swimming lazily around the boat. Some of the fish are three feet long.

Equally fascinating are the eruptions of sand at the bottom. That's where the spring water is coming from, through fissures in the limestone floor. Hard to believe, but the signs tell you that 10,000 gallons of water are pouring into Kitch-iti-kipi every minute.

It's always the same temperature, a constant forty-five degrees year-round. Great for the fish, not so great for human swimmers who are prohibited.

Kids will love it here. Who wouldn't? Dogs on a leash are welcome on the boat but they probably won't get much of a thrill out of it. Their eyesight's not all that great and they only see in black-and-white, right?

No cost. You just need a Recreation Passport on your vehicle.

Phone: 906-341-2355

Directions: From Thompson, take M-149 north for eight miles.

Thompson Fish Hatchery

Since the Upper Peninsula is considered a fisherman's paradise, it's good to know where these fish are coming from. Well, a lot of them–like a million a year–come from the Thompson State Fish Hatchery west of Manistique.

The hatchery, which raises Chinook salmon, steelhead trout and brown trout, is open seven days a week throughout the year, but be forewarned that June, July and August aren't the best months to visit. Most of the fish are released by late spring so the outside tanks, or "raceways," are empty during the summer.

This place is popular with hunters in November and with snowmobilers in December, January and February when the raceways are teeming with baby fish eager to exercise their fins out in the wild.

Still, there's plenty to see here year-round, including hands-on exhibits in the information center, a self-guided tour on the "yellow fish road" and a show pond featuring large, ponderous fish who somehow managed to escape the raceways during their time at the hatchery.

Groups of ten or more can arrange for guided tours. No cost.

Fishing poles are discouraged. And heck, who wants to catch a four-incher, anyway?

Address: 944 S M-149, Thompson

Phone: 906-341-5587

Directions: Drive on M-149 two miles north of US-2.

42

Fayette

Greece has the Parthenon, Peru has Macchu Picchu and the U.P. has…. Fayette Historic Township.

Okay, so you're not overly impressed. Granted, Fayette's not all that ancient but neither is the United States. Fayette was a self-contained community of 500 people from 1868 to 1891 where the workers manufactured pig iron while their families lived, shopped and went to school here.

It's located at the southern tip of the Garden Peninsula (part of the U.P.'s "banana belt") and it's a gorgeous, protected little harbor on Lake Michigan.

More than twenty of the town's buildings have been restored here, including some of the residences, both grand and humble, along with the hotel, the pay office, the barber shop, and the iron smelting operations.

If you visit, be prepared for a good, long walk. In the summertime, bring some water with you.

But it's worth it. You truly get a sense of what it was like to live and work in this isolated community on the southern coast of the Upper Peninsula.

Rover's allowed in Fayette as long as he's on a leash.

A Recreation Passport is needed.

If you want to arrive in style, you can bring your boat and dock here for a small fee.

Phone: 906-644-2603

Directions: Drive seventeen miles south of US-2 on county road 183.

Photo By Glenn Lamberg

Photo By Glenn Lamberg

Photo by Steve Gonde

Nahma Inn

You've heard the term "sleepy little town?" Well, Nahma is more like a comatose, little town. Until Saturday nights, when it comes alive at the Nahma Inn.

The inn used to be a hotel where the lumber barons put up their guests while doing business with them. Now it's been restored, complete with charming, inexpensive rooms, a quiet, tastefully decorated restaurant and an intimate, wood-panelled bar.

But come here on Saturday night and things get lively. In warm weather, sit out on the deck where you'll be entertained by bands or an occasional comedian or hypnotist. No cost, just order a beer or a glass of wine for a few bucks. Popcorn is free. Woohoo!

Summer nights are delightful here. There are worse ways to while away the hours. The neighbors at the next table might be from Chicago or Dallas or London or, heck….even Nahma.

When the weather gets cold or rainy, they bring you inside into the cozy little bar.

Bigtime fun in a tiny town that still boasts a post office but not much more.

The Nahma Inn is closed on Mondays.

Address: 13747 Main Street, Nahma

Phone: 906-644-2486

Website: www.nahmainn.com/

Peninsula Point Lighthouse

Talk about off the beaten path.

Peninsula Point Lighthouse (aka Peninsula Point Light) is a half hour south of US-2 at the southern tip of the Stonington Peninsula. The last two miles before you get to the lighthouse are a one lane dirt road with occasional turnouts to accommodate two-way traffic.

The best time to visit is September when monarch butterflies, with their pea-brains and their remarkable instincts, all gather here before resuming their migration south. A butterfly wonderland. Amazing.

But there's something else here, year-round, and if you have a ten-year-old with an interest in science, Peninsula Point Light is a must-see. Fossils up to 500 million years old are plentiful amid the rock and mud flats at the tip of this peninsula.

Bring a hammer and chisel with you, and unearth your treasures.

You can also climb the four story lighthouse here and settle in at a picnic table while sorting through your fossils or fending off the butterflies.

Rover's welcome to chase the butterflies.

Directions: From US-2 just east of Rapid River, take County Road 513 south for eighteen miles.

Ludington Park

This is one of the finest small town parks in the nation. It extends over 120 acres on one mile of Lake Michigan shoreline on the eastern tip of Escanaba.

It's the perfect place for an evening stroll or bike ride, summer, winter, spring or fall. Just dress appropriately.

Here's what you'll see: acres upon acres of grass and trees, a marina, a sandy beach, playgrounds, tennis courts, a lighthouse, a museum, a bandshell for summer concerts.

Bring your Frisbee here. Bring your dog. Bring your lover.

Take a nap in the shade or the sun.

Go to the entrance of the remarkably well protected harbor and watch the boats set out to sea or make their way back to shore.

The folks of Escanaba got it right years ago when they preserved this gorgeous hunk of land for a park on the edge of downtown. They're more than willing to share it with you.

Just don't get ticked off when you go home to your town's pocket park that's barely large enough for a rusty swing set, a rickety bench, a tiny garden and a plaque or two.

Directions: Drive east on Ludington Avenue or First through Seventh Avenues, until you run into the park.

Menominee First Street

Have you ever been to Ocean Drive on South Beach in Miami Beach?

Well, First Street in Menominee is just like Ocean Drive…except it doesn't have the hot weather, the hot women, the hot cars, and the suffocating crowds on the sidewalks and in the streets.

What it does have, however, is a gorgeous coastal location looking out on the bay of Green Bay, an expansive grassy park, and historic, well-preserved brick buildings.

Throw in a marina, a playground, a breakwater that you can walk on, and an overall freshness in the air and cleanliness on the ground, and you've got the perfect venue for a leisurely stroll, an invigorating jog, or an easy but entertaining bike ride.

If you get tired, take a break at the Serving Spoon, a bright, airy café that features fresh sandwiches, soups and espresso.

So no, First Street in Menominee really isn't much like South Beach, and for that, most Yoopers would say, "Thank God!"

Directions: From US-41, drive one mile east on 10th Avenue until you hit First Street and the water.

DeYoung Family Zoo

This isn't some big city zoo with clean, wide walkways, fancy cages, neatly manicured bushes, and popcorn and cotton candy stands around every corner, but it does have just about every kind of animal you'd ever want to see.

Five hundred of them total, from tigers and lions to camels and hyenas and monkeys, along with a hippo who goes by the name of Wallace. If you get to Wallace's habitat at lunch time, you might be able to feed him a watermelon. Whole. In one gulp. The big guy's got no manners.

The zoo is remote, rustic, dusty and unpretentious, to say the least, but you and the kids can wander here for a few hours and be thoroughly entertained. Watch for the feeding times. That's a lot of fun.

It's all the brain child of Bud DeYoung who started collecting the animals a few decades ago simply out of a love for them. Now the zoo and its inhabitants are an obsession for him. He's got a personal relationship with all of the animals.

Has he ever been attacked by any of them? "Not really," Bud replies. "Just some stitches here and there."

The DeYoung Family Zoo will cost you a little bit, twelve dollars for adults, less for children, and free for kids four and under.

But here's a guess: if you spent an entire week in the Upper Peninsula, your kids might say their fondest memory here was of this unique menagerie out in the middle of nowhere.

The zoo is open from April through October, then by appointment only during the winter. Call ahead.

Address: N5406 County Road 577, Wallace Phone: 906-788-4093

Website: www.thedeyoungfamilyzoo.com/

Directions: At the caution light in Wallace, fifteen minutes north of Menominee, go west on G-08 (aka CR 342) for a mile, then turn south on County Road 577. The zoo is a mile away.

48

Millie Mine Bats

If you get squeamish just thinking about bats, you might want to skip this venue. But seriously, you don't have to worry about these remarkable (but creepy) little guys somehow getting caught up in your hair and scaring the bejesus out of you.

They know what they're doing and they want nothing to do with you. Fifty thousand of them live in this 360 foot deep mine shaft covered by a grate atop Millie Hill in Iron Mountain, and if you want to watch them, the best time of the year is in late September before they go into hibernation.

Come here at dusk and take a seat at one of the benches around the shaft and wait for them to arrive. Quite a sight.

It can get chilly in late September, so bring a coat or a sweater, even a cup of coffee. It won't be the most romantic date you've ever been on, but it'll be a night to remember.

Four types of bats live here, all of them tiny, weighing no more than an ounce or two but, oh, those wings. Spooky.

While you're waiting for the bats to arrive, take a walk up the path to an overlook where you'll gaze at the town of Iron Mountain below and the Menominee Range beyond. A beautiful sight. Maybe that's why the bats chose to live here. No, wait. Bats are blind. Never mind.

Directions: From US-2 just north of downtown, go east on Second Street for three blocks, then turn right on Park Street and go to the top of the hill. It's there on the right.

Cornish Pump & Glider

This will cost you a little money–up to thirteen dollars for adults, much less for kids, but you'll get access to three museums in Iron Mountain: the Cornish Pump, the Glider exhibit, and the history museum.

The pump and the glider are technological dinosaurs but remarkable dinosaurs that will tell you something about this nation's history.

The pump, fifty-four feet high and weighing 725 tons, is one of the biggest ever built. It was used to drain the water out of the local mines in the late nineteenth and early twentieth centuries, but was then rendered obsolete when electric pumps took over.

Still. Just take a look at it. Utterly massive.

And then next door is the glider, one of about 4000 built by the Ford Motor Company in nearby Kingsford back in the Forties. These were the planes that flew American troops into France during the Normandy invasion in World War Two. No propellers, no engines. Just an efficient aerodynamic design that carried up to fifteen soldiers on board at eighty-five miles per hour.

The planes were technological marvels of their time. Gazing at the glider, you can't help but imagine what the troops were thinking– the anxiety and wonderment–as this massive craft transported them in utter silence across nighttime skies into enemy territory.

Phone: 906-774-1086

Directions: Just north of downtown on US-2, turn west on to Kent Street. It's up the hill about a quarter mile, on the left.

50

Pine Mountain Ski Jumps

All right, this little adventure demonstrates that the book's subtitle (that thing about being "free" or "cheap") is a little misleading. Well, actually, it's a lie. Go ahead, sue me.

The Pine Mountain Ski Jumps (aka the Continental Cup), which are held in February, are going to cost you. Twenty dollars for adults, fifteen for kids if you buy tickets in advance, and five dollars more per ticket if you buy on the day of the competition at Pine Mountain. The tickets are good for both Saturday and Sunday.

If you're a ski jumping aficionado and you're intensely curious about the keen competition between the Estonians and the Slovenians, this is a wonderful event. These guys, flying well over one hundred meters through the air, are world-class international ski jumpers.

But let's be honest, most of us don't know much about the sport. Our incisive analysis might amount to saying "Wow!" when we watch it.

The Pine Mountain Ski Jumps are more about the people on the ground, bundled up against the elements, holding a beer in one hand and hot dog in the other, with nachos on one side, and chocolate chip cookies on the other.

It's a monster tailgating party with 5000 of your closest friends.

And that's the thing: if you're going to fork out the twenty or twenty-five bucks, don't come alone. Make sure that you bring along a group of friends or family, along with a grill and lots of food and drink. Also plenty of warm clothes. Rover's welcome; just make sure he's warm.

You'll have a ball. And you might even learn a thing or two about ski jumping.

Address: N3332 Pine Mountain Road, Iron Mountain

Directions: From US-2/141, north of Iron Mountain, take Pine Mountain Road south about two miles. The jump is there on your left. You can't miss it.   Website: www.kiwanisskiclub.com/

Bond Falls

Bond Falls is neither as massive or popular as Tahquamenon Falls but here's what it does have: accessibility. You can actually walk next to the falls and dip your hand in the water.

Some of the steps near the top of the falls are wet because the falls frequently overflow their borders, so be careful.

This is a photographer's paradise any season of the year, including winter, because of the easy accessibility from bottom to top, on either side of the falls.

If you're not inclined to walking, the overlook is an easy five minute stroll from the parking lot. If you want to climb on a well-maintained path alongside the falls, it'll take you another ten minutes.

It's well worth it.

The water flows out of the Bond Stowage (reservoir) just a short distance away, down onto a basalt river bottom which then changes to sandstone downstream.

You're not going to get any closer to a waterfall anywhere.

Hang on to the kids, keep Rover on a leash.

Keep your camera dry.

A Recreation Passport is needed to park.

Directions: From Paulding on US-45, drive three miles east on Bond Falls Road. From M-28, just west of Trout Creek, take One Mile Road south which turns into Calderwood Road about six miles to the falls.

52

Paulding Light

Okay, so you're not one of those nut jobs who believes in ghosts and all that paranormal crap.

Well, here's a suggestion. Wait until it gets dark and then stop by the viewing site for the Paulding Light which is just about five miles north of Watersmeet.

What you'll see in the distance along the power line (One mile away? Three miles?) is a light that dims and brightens, dances to the left and right, up and down, occasionally turns almost red, and always enchants you. What the hell is it?

Legend has it that it's an Indian dancing on the power line, or the ghost of a long-ago mailman, or a lantern carrier who was killed by a train…or…who knows.

An investigative TV show went out here trying to figure it out and came away with no explanation. Some Michigan Tech spoilsports conducted their own investigation a while back and determined it had something to do with car headlights and taillights.

Bull.

It's unexplained and inexplicable, and a good way to spend part of an evening. You'll undoubtedly run into other curiosity-seekers out there, and they'll be snacking or imbibing, maybe warming themselves by a campfire. All of you will be entranced by the mesmerizing, dancing light.

Directions: Drive almost five miles north of Watersmeet on US-45 and you'll see a sign that says Robbins Pond Road. Take a left (west) there and go a half mile until you come to a barricade. That's the viewing spot.

Sylvania Wilderness

Some of the most extensive old-growth hardwood forests in the United States and some of the purest lakes are located here in the 18,000 acres of the Sylvania Wilderness.

No river runs through this huge tract of land where the Ojibwa used to live, so the thirty-four lakes here are spring-fed and untainted by run-off.

You can walk the twenty-five miles of trails at Sylvania and stay overnight at one of the eighty-four rustic campsites.

The United States Forest Service recognized the extraordinary value of this land when the agency bought it in 1967 and then proceeded to remove all buildings from it.

It's a wilderness, clean and fresh and pure and old.

If you hike, picnic or camp here, you'll be sharing the land with deer, bears, wolves, porcupines, bobcats, beavers, bald eagles and many more of their friends.

Leave them alone, pick up after yourself, and give thanks that we've been smart enough to preserve something like this.

Directions: From Watersmeet, drive west on US-2 three and a half miles, then take a left (south) on GCR 535. The entrance to the Wilderness is about three miles away.

Brian Cabell is the author of the novels *Flo the Flasher* and *Money in the Ground*, as well as *Portrait of a Peninsula*, a collaboration on the beauty and uniqueness of the Upper Peninsula with artist Paul Grant.

Brian is a veteran of thirty-five years in news broadcasting, including fourteen as a correspondent for CNN.

He was born in San Mateo, California and has lived in Marquette, Michigan since 2004.